In Memory of

BELLE SENNETT
Grandmother of Dan Sennett

Donated by:
HIAWATHA PTA

Marco Polo

Marco Polo

BY
JON NOONAN

ILLUSTRATED BY YOSHI MIYAKE

CRESTWOOD HOUSE
NEW YORK

Maxwell Macmillan Canada
Toronto

Maxwell Macmillan International
New York   Oxford   Singapore   Sydney

To Lawrence and Ilse Maldarelli
with special thanks.

CRESTWOOD HOUSE
Macmillan Publishing Company
866 Third Avenue, New York, NY 10022

Maxwell Macmillan Canada, Inc.
1200 Eglinton Avenue East, Suite 200
Don Mills, Ontario M3C 3N1

Macmillan Publishing Company is part of the
Maxwell Communication Group of Companies

First Edition
Book design by Sylvia Frezzolini
Printed in the United States of America

10 9 8 7 6 5 4 3 2 1

LIBRARY OF CONGRESS CATALOGING-IN-PUBLICATION DATA
Noonan, Jon.
Marco Polo / by Jon Noonan. — 1st ed.
p.   cm. — (Explorers)
Includes Index.
Summary: Describes the life and journeys of the Italian trader who became famous for his travels in Asia.
ISBN 0-89686-704-8
1. Polo, Marco, 1254–1323?—Journeys—Juvenile literature. 2. Voyages and travels—Juvenile literature. 3. Explorers—Italy—Biography—Juvenile literature. 4. China—Discovery and travel—to 1900—Juvenile literature. [1. Polo, Marco, 1254–1323? 2. Explorers. 3. Voyages and travels.] I. Title. II. Series: Noonan, Jon. Explorers.
G370.P9A6 1993   91–33487
915.04′2′092—dc20
[B]

CONTENTS

THE TRAVELS OF MARCO POLO

Too Hot

It was too hot. The giant sun seemed to cover half the sky. Although it was springtime the scorching sunshine made people feel like they were standing on a stove. In the summer it would get even worse.

Marco Polo and everyone else in the city left for cooler ground. They moved many miles away to some streams found on the inner plain of the desert.

Trying to cross Asia in the 1200s, Marco Polo stayed for a while by these streams in southern Persia. With his father and uncle, Marco Polo traded goods from faraway countries. The city they had been visiting, Hormuz, was a trading center.

Besides the sun, something else gave them cause to go to the streams. The traders feared the super-hot summer winds called **simooms.** Like a fast fire the simooms raced across the sands, suffocating and roasting everything in their way.

Cool water and safety came from the streams. The streams had huts built over them. The huts were staked into the sandy shoulders and bottoms of the streams.

One summer day, the traders were extra grateful for the waterways. Sometime before noon the simooms came. Everyone jumped into the streams.

At this same time several thousand soldiers were traveling to the city to see the king of Hormuz. They were sent by the king of Kerman to collect gifts and **tribute.**

As they came close to the city, the soldiers were caught away from water in the summer winds. The strong waves of heat and flying sand struck them at full force.

On and on for hours the simooms soared across the sand. As the sizzling sunshine baked their bodies the skin of the soldiers started to crack. The giant, glaring sun and the superheated simooms began to cook them alive.

Meanwhile, Marco and the other traders huddled under their huts, up to their chins in the streams, as the hot winds stormed by the front of their faces.

Later, the winds went away. The soldiers were found suffocated on the sand. The city traders dug trenches far to the side of the soldiers. Then they tried to pull the soldiers by the arms to bury them. The soldiers were so baked and dried that their arms came off their bodies. New trenches had to be dug next to where each soldier had fallen.

Marco the Explorer

Soon after these events, Marco Polo continued his travels into other lands. Some of the trips would be nicer, and others would threaten his life again.

Marco Polo told the story of his travels to his writer friend Rustichello. Rustichello wrote, "I would have you know that, from the creation of Adam to the present day, no . . . other person of whatever . . . generation, explored so many parts of the world, or saw such wonders, as this Messer Marco Polo."

YOUNG MARCO POLO

Marco as a Boy

Marco Polo's own story began in 1254, when he was born in the Italian seacoast city of Venice. His father Nicolo Polo traded goods in cities far from home. He was away on business when Marco was born.

Sometime in the first 15 years of his life, Marco's mother died. His father had still not returned. Some relatives of the family lived in Venice. It is thought that they took care of Marco after his mother's death.

The **Catholic church** was one of two centers of social life in Venice. Nearly everyone attended church celebrations and services. Seven special times in the day were saved for prayer and worship. Marco's **Christian** education shows in his stories. He was probably educated at the Church of Saint Mark like other children in the city.

Saint Mark's Church

Saint Mark was a special saint to Venice. Like Marco many boys in the city were named after him. Completed in the 11th century, the giant Church of Saint Mark still stands today. It is located on the east side of Saint Mark's Square, which is in the center of the city.

The church is several stories high. Four horse statues stand on an upper level high above the arched entrance.

Inside Marco and other visitors could see the five large domes on the ceiling set in the shape of a cross. Scenes from the Bible, such as the paired animals of Noah and his ark, are shown on the walls and ceiling.

City of Traders

The second center of social life was trade. Goods from other lands were unloaded from **galleys** at the wharf. Then these goods were brought into the city on narrow canal boats. The central channel was the Grand Canal. About two miles long, this waterway still winds its way through Venice

today, separating the city into two almost equal halves.

Like other children of traders Marco likely visited the boat workers on the canals and the traders at the wharf. There is also a good chance that he looked for his father to come home.

Father Comes Home

Then at age 15, Marco saw his father for the first time. Nicolo told Marco about his long travels in search of trade goods. He had gone to the East, seeking silk, spices, gems, gold and other treasures. When Marco learned how his father had journeyed all the way to Cathay (northern China), he started to understand that such trips could take several years.

Just as Marco would in the future, Nicolo and his brother Maffeo had visited the Great Khan, who lived in Cathay. This title meant "great lord" or "leader of all other lords." The empire of the Great Khan was huge. His lands stretched thousands of miles across Asia, from China to the edges of Europe.

The Great Khan told the Polo brothers he wished to learn more about the Christian faith. He accepted all faiths in his kingdom, but he wanted to know which one was the best.

He asked Nicolo and Maffeo to go to Christ's

tomb where a lamp filled with holy oil was said to be eternally lit. The Khan wished for a sample of this oil. He also requested that the **Pope,** the leader of the Christian church, be asked to send a hundred **missionaries** to Cathay. They were to teach their knowledge of Christ. If the missionaries could show why their faith was stronger than all others, then the Great Khan and all his people would convert to the Christian faith.

The Gold Tablet

The Great Khan gave Nicolo and Maffeo a gold tablet. The tablet commanded all the officers in the empire to help the two travelers on their way. Everywhere they went, on showing the tablet, the traders were treated with honor and given whatever they needed. The Polos returned as far as Acre, now in the state of Israel, in April 1269.

Acre was a city in Biblical lands open to all Christians, thanks to the Crusades. In the Crusades of the 11th, 12th and 13th centuries, knights and other Christians came to save these lands for others of their faith. Acre was one of the cities in which they were successful for a time.

While there the Polos learned that Pope Clement IV had died just a few months earlier. They

would have to wait until a new Pope was chosen by the Catholic **cardinals.**

In the meantime the brothers returned to Venice where Nicolo found his son. Marco wished he could travel with his father. Two years later he got his wish.

MARCO GETS TO GO

In 1271, Nicolo and Maffeo decided to return to the Great Khan before too much time passed. They let Marco, now 17 years old, come with them.

For the first part of their trip the traders purchased passage on a galley. When the wind blew too lightly on the sail, the crew would take to their long oars to continue the voyage. Sea battles with ships from the city of Genoa were common. For safety, the galleys sailed with a convoy of other trading ships. The ships were sturdy but crowded.

The convoy voyaged across the sea to Acre. Landing safely, the Polos saw Teald, an agent of the former Pope. They asked for his permission to take some of the oil from the lamp at Christ's tomb. He approved their request and they continued on to Jerusalem.

The Holy Oil

The three travelers came to the spot where Christ had been laid and saw the lighted lamp. They took a sample of the holy oil and returned to Acre. Teald gave the traders letters that stated they had tried to fulfill all the Great Khan's requests but that a new pope still needed to be chosen.

The Polos traveled by boat to Laias, a city in Greater Armenia, now southern Turkey, that traded in silk cloths and spices. While they were there, a messenger sent by Teald informed them of a new pope. Teald himself had been elected. He chose the name Pope Gregory X. He invited the Polos to see him soon in Acre. Marco said they gladly made the return voyage in a galley prepared for them by the king of Greater Armenia.

The new pope chose only two of his churchmen, both friars, to accompany the Polos on their journey to Cathay. He also gave the friars letters and messages for the Great Khan. The Polos then returned to Laias, bringing the friars with them.

They found the area under threat of attack from Egyptian armies coming up through nearby

Syria. The two friars wanted to be safe and go home. They gave letters to the Polos and left the city in the company of some Christian knights. The Polos continued onward.

The Edge of the Empire

Soon, the traders were in lands ruled by leaders of the Khan empire. The Polos still had their gold tablet of the Great Khan with them. They also joined **caravans** of other travelers, riding horses, camels and sometimes donkeys.

Passing through Armenia and Turcomania (now Anatolia, the Asian part of Turkey), Marco took note of high Mount Ararat, where remains of Noah's ark were said to still exist. He said the mountain was topped with high snows and was too hard to climb at the time. In the 20th century climbers said they found very old wood on the top that may have come from the ark.

Marco saw shepherds who made their clothing and houses out of animal skins. He also spoke of the great fountains of oil found west of the Caspian Sea. The oil was good for fuel and for treating camels with skin irritations.

The Polos continued their journey into Yrak (called Iraq today) and Persia (now called Iran). In these countries they found many items of trade including fine cloths of silk and gold.

Most of the people in these lands were **Muslims.** Some were Christians. According to Marco some of the Muslim leaders did not like Christians. In trying to make their lands Muslim only they often put to death anyone who did not agree with their faith.

The edges of the Khan empire were not always under control. As a Christian Marco had to be very careful in these lands. The Polos circled around a war in Syria and reached Persia safely. In southern Persia however, they came upon new troubles.

Travel to the Coast

After they reached the city of Kerman the Polo family traveled toward the coast. They heard they would find a trading center of fine goods there. The Polos may have hoped also to find a ship to take them to the east more quickly.

Leaving Kerman, the Polos and their long caravan of fellow traders found the first days traveling to be pleasant. They felt safe being together in large numbers. All carried weapons such as arrows, bows and knives for hunting and protection. They saw towns and strong forts along the way. Several kinds of birds and wild animals were also sighted.

After seven days of going slowly up a slope the

Polos came to the top of a tall mountain. It was extremely cold there. Even several layers of clothing could not keep out the chill.

They took two days to ride down the other side. No more towns were sighted. They saw only a few shepherds with their flocks of sheep.

A wide plain spread before them as they reached the mountain bottom. Castles and towns surrounded by walls of earth were seen.

The days grew hot again. The distance to cross the plain was about a five-day journey. Along the way Marco saw humped oxen with smooth hair as white as snow. The oxen were taught by their owners to kneel like camels. After goods were loaded on their backs, the animals would rise again.

As the traders' caravan came closer to the sea-coast a fog slowly spread over the land. It grew so thick that nothing could be seen.

Trouble with Thieves

A cunning tribe of thieves had waited for the fog to come. They did not race toward the caravan screaming and waving their swords. Instead they rode slowly and silently through the fog to catch the travelers up close. They spread across the plain so as not to miss any section of the long caravan.

Suddenly screams of surprise could be heard from the caravan. The sword-wielding thieves attacked. The Polos and their companions fought for their lives.

Somehow Marco escaped with great speed to the castle of Canosalmi. His father and uncle also reached safety. When the gloom cleared only a handful of survivors were found. All the rest had been killed or taken to be sold as slaves. Their goods had been taken as well. The thieves were called Karaunas.

The Polos continued their journey across the hot desert. Luckily they still had their gifts and letters from the Pope. At the end of the plain they traveled down a rocky trail to a lower level. Here Marco saw sparkling streams and gardens. It was a welcome sight. After two days of travel the traders came to the ocean. There they saw the harbor of Hormuz. The Polos had arrived in southern Persia.

The Trading Center

It was not yet springtime. Marco saw ships from India carrying cargoes of spice, silk, pearls, gems and elephant tusks. Hormuz was a large and busy trading center. Arabian horses were traded and loaded for the return trip. But Marco was not happy with the ships.

He thought the ships were very weak. Many were said to fall apart at sea. They were secured with only thread and pieces of wood instead of iron nails. There were no decks on the ships. The Arabian horses had to travel standing on top of the other goods. The Polos wanted their goods as well as themselves to be safe and not stepped on or lost at sea.

Marco was not happy with the hot weather there, either. Everyone left the city before the start of summer. It was then that the scorching simooms caused everyone to jump in the streams on the inner plain.

The Polos soon chose to return to Kerman, this time bypassing the trail that led to the Karaunas.

They enjoyed this route better. Along the way there were many hot springs. The hot baths were said to help cure skin diseases and itches. A lot of fruit and dates were found also.

The Empty Land

Going north from Kerman was a different story. The hot, dry desert seemed empty. No animals were seen, and there was nothing for the traders to eat. The only water they found on the trail was salty and as green as grass. Even a single drop made them sick. Luckily the Polos carried some water in containers.

The small caravan journeyed for two days through the desert. The travelers and their beasts of burden were hot and dry. Their thirsty horses drank the bitter green water and suffered severely. On the third day it was still the same—endless empty sand, extreme heat and no fresh water.

On the fourth day a stream appeared on the sand from an underground source. The water was clean and good to drink.

So the Polos continued through the desert. Some days were hot and dry. On others they found water and, sometimes, villages. Marco became sick for a long time on this trip. When he came to the clean air and water of the mountains however, he got better right away.

The High Mountains

The Polos reached the northern edge of what is now Afghanistan. They came to the high mountains of Pamir to the north and Kashmir to the south.

Marco learned about the mountain **monks** of Kashmir, who were said to live very long lives. They ate little food and tried to keep themselves free of all wrongdoing.

In the Pamir, some of the peaks are more than 20,000 feet high. The people living there called the

land the roof of the world. Marco learned of a beautiful meadow and lake found between two of the highest mountains.

Thin animals were said to grow fat on the fine pasture. Among the animals seen there, Marco spoke of large wild sheep with giant horns. Today these sheep are called *Ovis Poli* (Polo's sheep) in his honor.

The Polos continued onward for several months. Marco found some village people in the lands they visited to be friendly and others mean. Some were strong-looking and healthy. Others were diseased or disfigured. But always the countryside was beautiful, challenging or both. The traders explored many mountains and plains until they came to the city of Lop on the edge of a desert, the Taklimakan in west China.

The Great Spirit Desert

Stories of magic surrounded this great desert. If visitors became lost spirits would come. Sometimes the spirits made sounds like drums and other musical instruments. Other times the spirits sounded like friends calling the lost ones to safety.

Sometimes imaginary visions of caravans, lakes or armies were seen far away. The lost visitors followed the sights and sounds wherever they led.

Alone, away from their caravan, their water and food soon gave out. Their bleached bones could be seen scattered over this giant desert. Its size was so great that its most narrow part could not be crossed in less than 30 days.

Centuries later people found that the sights and sounds were made by natural effects of the sand, heat and wind, and not spirits. Marco said he heard some of the sounds himself and thought them wonderful.

Before trying to cross this desert, the Polos first rested in Lop for a week. Then they gathered food and supplies and began the crossing with a small caravan. The traders were told that water could be found in the desert, but only enough for a company of 50 people and their pack animals.

The caravan kept close together. Before sleeping they marked the direction they had to travel. The Polos also tied bells to their camels and donkeys so the animals would not get separated from them.

Luckily, the travelers found water holes spaced about a day apart. All but three or four out of the 28 places they found had good water available. After 30 days their crossing was completed safely.

Day by day the Polos came closer to Cathay. While they were still weeks away from the Great

Khan, soldiers saw them and raced on horseback to tell the news to their lord.

The Great Khan was glad to hear that the Polos were coming. He sent a group of people to greet them.

THE GREAT KHAN

The Great Khan was now at his summer palace in a place called the City of Peace. Like all the palaces he built, the grounds and buildings were beautiful.

The lands of the Great Khan formed the largest empire the earth had ever known. First conquered by Mongol and Tartar warriors led by Genghis Khan in the early 1200s, the empire eventually came under the control of his grandson. This grandson expanded the empire into southern China in the 1270s. Named Kublai, the grandson became known as the Great Khan.

The Polos arrived in the city in 1275 and were guided to the Great Khan. Entering the giant palace, they found him in the company of 12,000 barons, his chosen men. Marco, Nicolo and Maffeo knelt before the Great Khan, touching their foreheads to the floor.

The Great Khan had them rise and stand upright. He treated them with honor and showed gladness at the return of the two brothers. He asked them questions about their travels and gave them all a great feast.

Nicolo and Maffeo gave the Great Khan the letters from the Pope and the gift of holy oil from Jerusalem. The Khan thanked the Polos for their faithfulness. Seeing the young man in their group the Great Khan asked about Marco.

Marco recalled his father saying to the Great Khan, "He is my son and your liege man." A liege man is one who is loyal to a king.

The Great Khan was pleased and made Marco an honored member of his household. The Polos stayed at the Great Khan's court and were honored above even his barons.

Marco stayed at court and learned the language and customs of the Mongols. He learned to read and write in four languages of the Khan's kingdom. After two years, he was made an **agent** of the Great Khan. Marco traveled to many parts of the kingdom, often with his father and uncle, and performed services for the Great Khan.

The Cathay Capital

The Great Khan liked to celebrate each new year at his wonderful winter palace. It stood in Cathay's **capital,** which was called the Lord's City.

The Great Khan's castle was surrounded by high walls of earth several miles long. Inside the Khan constructed a planned city. Handsome houses and lovely gardens were built along several straight streets.

To the south stood the Great Khan's palace, surrounded by its own set of castle walls and gates. Its giant roof shone like crystal and could be seen from miles away.

A large lake and lovely forest came close to the palace. Every time the Great Khan was informed of a beautiful tree growing somewhere in his kingdom, he ordered it dug up, with all its roots and the earth around it. Then it was brought to his forest on the backs of elephants.

Close to China's current capital of Beijing, the Lord's City was about 30 miles (a day's journey) south of the Great Wall. The Great Wall, which had been completed in 200 B.C., was then almost 1,200 miles long.

The Celebration

Among the guests who came to the new year celebration was Marco Polo. Once simply a trader,

Marco now lived as a special member of the Great Khan's court.

Everyone dressed in white clothes for the occasion. The Great Khan's people, the Mongols, thought of white as the color of joy and good fortune. From all over the empire, the guests of the Khan entered the Lord's City, expanding the gathering into the tens of thousands.

From a high view, the Great Khan watched as 100,000 white horses and other gifts passed before his eyes. Five thousand of the emperor's elephants, each carrying two treasure chests filled with gold cups and other things necessary for a holiday feast, were then unloaded. A great number of camels covered with white silk cloth, also carried items for the celebration. Then the great feast began.

A great variety of beasts, birds and fish were served. The palace hall was large enough for 6,000 people to sit inside for the feast. A gold drinking cup was given to everyone. More than 40,000 additional guests were fed on the grounds close to the hall.

The Great Khan could see them all from his high throne. All the male members of his household sat to his right. His first wife (the empress) and all the other female family members sat to his left. The 12,000 barons came dressed in white robes so finely made, they looked like kings.

Every time the Great Khan held his cup up to take a drink, musical instruments were sounded and all present fell on their knees to honor their lord. When the feast ended, the emperor's entertainers then performed for the entire gathering.

Marco Explores Cathay

Marco served the Great Khan for 17 years. In that time, the trader traveled to nearly all of the lands around Cathay and saw great Chinese cities, statues and other sights.

He went on hunting trips with the Great Khan, saw giant serpents (called crocodiles today) with tiny legs and eyes as big as round bread loaves, learned of **lamas** who lived all their lives on bran and water, saw rivers filled with thousands of Chinese boats and met friendly people in faraway villages.

Marco also saw paper money for the first time, traveled on tree-lined roads that led to the Cathay capital, voyaged across the ocean to visit India, saw pony express riders who delivered messages across Cathay, and explored rich trading centers and beautiful temples.

The time came, however, when the Polos became homesick. Nicolo spoke to the Great Khan about their wish to return to Venice. At first the

Great Khan said no. He liked the services of the Polos too much to let them go.

Only when he had no other choice did the Great Khan say yes. Some of his agents tried to bring a princess to Persia to be married to a Khan leader. The agents found too much fighting in the central Asian lands, so they asked to go by sea. Of all the Great Khan's people, only the Polos were thought to have enough ocean experience for the long voyage.

THE VOYAGE HOME

The Polos and the princess rode with hundreds of passengers and crew on large Chinese sailing ships. They voyaged to Sumatra and India on the way to Persia.

In Sumatra, Marco saw unicorns almost as big as elephants. Each one had a long, thick horn coming out of its head. A unicorn like this creature can still be seen today. People call it a rhinoceros. He also saw nuts as large as human heads. Today we call them coconuts.

On the coast of India Marco saw lots of teenage traders. They were expected to earn their living from age 13. They often traded in pearls that were brought in from the sea. Up the coast, Marco also learned of special valleys where lots of diamonds could be found.

In Persia, the Polos left the princess safe in her new kingdom. They left their ship and made their way home to Venice.

On the way, they learned that the Great Khan had died. Within a century, the Khan empire would split into separate kingdoms and the trade routes across Asia would close to outsiders.

When Marco, Nicolo and Maffeo first came back to Venice, people thought they were poor strangers. Only when they opened their ragged clothes to show great gems and other treasures from their travels did their friends accept them as the long-lost Polos. It was then 1295. They had been gone for 24 years.

Soon after his arrival, Marco was asked to captain one of several galleys for a sea battle against the city of Genoa. Marco said yes. The sailors of Genoa won. Marco was captured. As a prisoner of war Marco was sent to jail in Genoa.

Here, Marco met a fellow prisoner who was a writer. To pass the time Marco spoke of his travels. The writer liked Marco's stories. They agreed to make a book together.

The writer wrote in French and gave his name as Rustacians. It is thought today that his Italian name was Rustichello. While Marco spoke Rustichello wrote everything he said.

In 1299 Genoa agreed to free war prisoners.

Marco got out of jail and returned to Venice. He called his completed book *The Description of the World*.

Marco soon married. He and his wife, Donata, had three daughters. Marco lived to about age 70. He died in early 1324 leaving his wife an income for life in his will.

Marco Inspires Others

Marco's book was hand copied and thus spread across Europe. Two centuries later, it was printed in large quantities by printing presses.

The book was read by European royalty. Explorers such as Christopher Columbus and **Vasco da Gama** read it too. On their voyages these explorers tried to find new ocean routes to the wondrous lands Polo described.

His stories of adventure and riches helped inspire a new era of exploration. Marco's words opened the minds of others to a wider world.

GLOSSARY

agent—A person who acts for another person.

Buddhist—One who believes in the teachings of Buddha, who was born in the 6th century B.C. in India.

capital—City where a country's leaders act and rule.

caravan—Group of people traveling together.

cardinals—The highest Catholic church leaders except for the Pope.

Catholic church—The Christian church that is headed by the Pope.

Christian—One who believes in the teachings of Jesus Christ, who was born in the 1st century.

galley—Large and low medieval ship propelled by sails and oars and used in the Mediterranean for war and trading.

lamas—Priests of the Buddhist faith in Tibet.

missionaries—People sent by their church to teach others.

monks—Men who live apart from the world to follow their religion.

Muslim—One who believes in the teachings of Muhammad, an Arab prophet born in the 6th century, A.D.

Pope—The leader of the Catholic church. The first Pope was Saint Peter, an apostle of Jesus in the 1st century A.D.

simoom—A hot, dry, violent dust-laden wind from Asia or Africa.

tribute—Taxes, goods or money paid to a strong ruler or king.

Vasco da Gama—Explorer who voyaged around Africa to India.

INDEX